What if you could?

- Find inspiration and stop feeling stuck
- Thrive both personally and professionally
- Find purpose and larger meaning in what you do
- Have positive thoughts that push you into momentum
- Surround yourself with people that propel you
- Have a mindset of abundance and resilience

What if you could?

The Mindset and Business Blueprint for Your Life of Purpose

written by these guys

Cody May / Neil Morton

What If You Could? The Mindset And Business Blueprint For Your Life of Purpose
Published by StudioPTBO Inc.
Peterborough, Ontario, Canada

MAY, CODY, and MORTON, NEIL, Authors
WHAT IF YOU COULD?
CODY MAY and NEIL MORTON

ISBN: 978-1-7775546-0-6 (Paperback)
ISBN: 978-1-7775546-1-3 9 (Ebook)

BUSINESS & ECONOMICS / Entrepreneurship
SELF-HELP / Personal Growth / Success

QUANTITY PURCHASES: Schools, companies, professional groups, clubs,
and other organizations may qualify for special terms when
ordering quantities of this title.
For information, email Info@StudioPTBO.com.

DEDICATION

To my parents, Randy and Lisa, my sister Candice, her husband Aaron and my niece Ava Grace: thank you for always believing in me. Thank you also to my mentor, Robert Gauvreau, for presenting me with my most memorable opportunity on my entrepreneurial journey.

-Cody May

To my wife and best friend, Christi; my daughters, Avery and Chloe; my parents Patricia and David; sister, Denise; and in-laws, Harry and Bonnie—thanks to all of you for always being there for me and inspiring me to no end.

-Neil Morton

CONTENTS

FOREWORD

Your perspective is what shapes the world around you, which is why having the right perspective is so essential if you want to be happy, healthy, and successful in your pursuits. I'm a believer that there is a very simple equation for what some people like to call luck. Your attention (or what you're aware of) plus your intention (or what you think, say, do, and believe) equals the coincidences that happen in your life. That's the two-variable equation for luck!

When you set the priorities for what you want, either personally or professionally, you need to have intention—the mindset that pushes you toward what you want. When you live as a person in consistent and persistent pursuit of your potential, I believe you can have the best intentions, but those intentions will not always be able to carry you through to success. If you don't pay enough attention to how closely your actions are aligned with your core values, you will find happiness to be elusive.

When someone is not putting their attention and intention on values such as gratitude, empathy, accountability, and effective communication, they are much more prone to missteps and mistakes.

Unfortunately, most people make mistakes with good intent, which means that fixing the mistakes requires much more attention and work to re-engineer actions, allowing them to align with our core values.

Attention allows you to take your intention—that is, a possibility in your life—and put clarity, balance, and focus towards accomplishing it. Focus brings attention and inspiration—and inspiration is timeless. When you're inspired, it feels like there is no such thing as time. Have you ever watched a movie, speech, or some other long-form content that was very inspirational? You say, "Whoa. That was two and a half hours? It felt like just a few minutes." And have you ever seen a cinematic disaster that feels like it takes two and a half weeks to get through? The difference was that you were emotionally involved and invested in those inspirational TV shows, movies, podcasts, and speeches. They're timeless.

Despite the popularity of the phrase, it is important to know that practice does not make perfect. It's a deliberate practice, with both intention and attention, that allows you to steadily progress with whatever skills you're looking to improve. Utilize the power of intention every day to gain the skills you need to effect change in your life. Taking stock of the reasons that you want to make the change is a great place to start, then look to your intentions and realize where you can improve. You need to give your skills your attention and focus every single day to yield your desired results.

Many of us also fail to realize that what we pay attention to and give intention to, will create coincidences in our life, regardless of whether we want them or not. When we put our attention and intention on the "wrong things", those negative coincidences occur. That is why elevating our awareness and strengthening our mindset with books like *What If You Could?* is so vital. The lessons contained within will help to ensure you pay attention to and give intention to the right things, so that luck or the right coincidences occur in your life.

David Meltzer
Co-Founder, Sports 1 Marketing

PROLOGUE

YOU MAKE YOUR OWN LUCK IN LIFE

Ransacked. Our agency headquarters, both floors. Every piece of our prized video equipment stolen, about $10,000 worth. Doesn't sound like much, but for a startup like us, crushing. You want to cry, but you just have to fight.

The police came, looked at our surveillance footage (nothing but hoodie), dusted for fingerprints, and managed expectations.

They were like, *Listen we're busy. We might be able to hit up the pawn shops later in the week but if you guys have the time, best you head over there right away with your serial numbers and cross your fingers they turn up here, not at an out-of-town shop.*

We (Cody and Neil, the authors of this book) thought, *Let's go!* Knowing it would be like winning the lottery, we hit up every one of the downtown pawn shops. At the last shop—literally at the moment we're giving our serial numbers to the clerk—a guy walks in and stands next to us. And what do you know? He's weighed down by a heavy knapsack, our camera lens popping out.

We look at each other, thinking, *What are the odds?* Signaling the clerk to stall the dude, we head outside and call the police officer, *Get over here!* We're sharing the sidewalk with the thief's spotter.

After an eternity (less than five minutes), one cop pulls up, then another, sirens blaring. Like a Netflix thriller, traffic backs up at the nearest intersection and passers-by gawk in wonderment.

As the cop nears the pawn shop, the thief makes a run for it while his spotter bolts in the other direction. The cop chases the bad guy (and our gear) while Neil chases the cop chasing the bad guy (and our gear). Luckily, the cop caught the thief first.

The long and short of our story is:

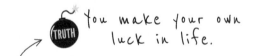
You make your own luck in life.

Pssst. Keep your eyes peeled for these truth bombs throughout the book. It's the good stuff we wish someone had told us earlier.

Our kind of luck begins with an action-oriented mindset that is all about going after life and business, not waiting for it to come to you. It is driven by starting, trying, being resilient, and never giving up.

This book is a blueprint for building your life of purpose. In it are the principles, attitudes, and mindsets we live by and that have brought us success and joy. We hope they will inspire you and make a big difference in your life.

We invite you to read our book front to back, back to front, or start in the middle; there is no real order. But the way to get the most value from our book is to mull over what you've read, make notes, dog-ear the pages and revisit them often, try out the principles and mindsets for yourself, and share them with family, friends, and colleagues.

Turn the page, and let's dive in.

$\longrightarrow$

MINDSET

JUST START

One of our office doors features a Latin phrase, *Memento Mori,* which means *It is inevitable that we die.* This mindset drives us to bring our best each day because life is finite.

Start by starting. Don't talk about what you're going to do tomorrow or someday. Do it now. Get on the treadmill. Crack the spine of that book. Put pen to paper in that journal. Put shovel to dirt for that garden. Build a bucket list for your life and business and get busy crossing off things.

Don't put off stuff until this afternoon, tomorrow, or next month. Don't tell yourself you're going to do that next spring or before you turn 50. Do it now. Tomorrow may never come, so embrace today.

Retrain your brain muscle to act now and get out of procrastination mode. The more "reps" you do, the more things you complete and cross off your list, the greater the rush you'll get from accomplishing things.

Just for now, close this book and start that project you've always wanted to do. You are not promised tomorrow.

Dog-ear this page to hold your spot, and come back to us later.

FOLD HERE

Well... what are you waiting for?
We weren't kidding. Close this book and go start
that project you've always wanted to do.

START WITH GRATITUDE

We look at gratitude as a mindset, a perspective, a healthy outlook on life. When you begin every day in a place of gratitude, that mindset begins to shift your attitude.

We've found that the best place to start with gratitude is simply to be thankful for the breath in our lungs.

As you read this book, we encourage you to stop and take just five minutes to breathe and simply express gratitude and appreciation for life.

Viktor Frankl, author of *Man's Search for Meaning,* said,

"Everything can be taken from a man but one thing: the last of the human freedoms—to choose one's attitude in any given set of circumstances, to choose one's own way."

Despite our circumstances, we have the power to choose our attitude. We have a choice to see the glass as half-full or half-empty. Try to focus on what you have rather than on what you don't have.

It's impossible to live your best life when filled with negativity, cynicism, and angst.

Make the choice to start with gratitude and express appreciation for life every day.

Believe
IN AFFIRMATIONS

Will yourself to believe that what you want will come true. Get a tattoo that says so, put it on a sticky or your whiteboard, record yourself saying it, say it to others. Repeat and lather in it.

Repeated affirmations sustain a focused mindset, one that propels you to carry on until the things you believe are actualized. When you truly believe, your affirmations will become reality.

Said another way, we become what we focus on and practice. Think about it: any positive, life-altering experience in your life most likely started with positive self-talk, even if it was subconscious.

Brendon Burchard teaches many of the world's highest performers to use affirmations or I AM statements to gain clarity and live extraordinary lives.

So, what do you want out of life? Most entrepreneurs start their business for one of three reasons: more money, more meaning, or more freedom. For Cody, it was a mixture of all three. Entrepreneurship showed him that opportunities are endless and there are no ceilings, except the ones you limit yourself to.

If you want more money, we encourage you to visualize yourself with that money. See your company crossing the $1 million revenue mark, then $3 million, then $5 million. Envision at each revenue mark who you need to be, what you are wearing, the car you are driving, the books you have read, and with whom you are spending your time. Lean into the feeling of who that person is and step into their shoes daily.

So many try to chase the outcome, but when you stop and examine those who have led extraordinary lives, you realize they chased the person they needed to become to achieve the outcome they desired.

MERITOCRACY WINS THE DAY

Our experience proves that when you give your team members all the tools they need to succeed, those with the ability and willingness to perform at high levels will succeed.

This is why everyone doesn't deserve equal raises and promotions. When you reward and promote your team based on their willingness to drive results (not their CV or tenure), your company will grow exponentially.

This approach doesn't mean you're unkind or a mean boss; business is a competition, not a country club.

Let the cream of the crop rise to the top.

NOT EVERYONE GETS A TROPHY

404 Error
Trophy
Not Found

The world is competitive. It's not a festival where everyone wins an award or gets a ribbon for participating. Nor should it be, as that would teach children and adults nothing.

To win, you need to be mentally and physically strong, committed to continuous improvement, and recognize, as the great Kobe Bryant did with his "mamba mentality," that the journey is the process and the process never ends.

To position yourself to win, you must be more resilient, more competitive, have more grit, and practice harder than your competition.

WHY DOESN'T THE CEREAL GO ON TOP?

There are too many silly habits and rules in life. Question them.

Don't conform to what everyone else is doing or do it the way it's always been done. Make the right decision for you and your company, regardless.

Innovation, individuality, and self-expression are often hampered by a heavy rule book.

So, colour outside the lines. Wear white clothing well into the fall. Eat eggs for dinner. Beta test that idea your team member threw out during a coffee walk.

Pour your cereal on top of the milk
— it stays "crispier" longer.

JOIN THE BOOK CLUB

There was a moment early on in our agency when Neil told Cody, "You really need to start reading books."

"I'm not a reader." Cody ignored the prompt, but not for long. Because this was the same guy who took Neil's earlier advice to "Network your ass off," which changed his life and business fortunes forever.

 Network your ass off.

Cody began reading books. Check that—Cody began devouring books—now, over 60 a year. Business books, leadership books, marketing books, branding books, biographies, history books. You name it, he's read it. No question that reading has positively impacted the direction of Cody's life and the direction of our business.

The more you read (hey, you're reading this, right?), the more you learn. Clue: the average CEO reads 52 books a year.

 Success leaves clues.

We really believe one of the primary reasons people fail or haven't succeeded yet is because they just haven't discovered the information they need.

If you want a breakthrough in your life and business, read more.

At first, you may have to push yourself to read, but once you adopt the mindset of a life-long learner, it will become fun, not homework.

Recommend valuable books to others. Trade books with colleagues and business friends regularly. You'll gain a lot of wisdom from reading and discussing them.

Read and learn from the best; there's gold in every book. All smart, successful people read books. And eventually write one.

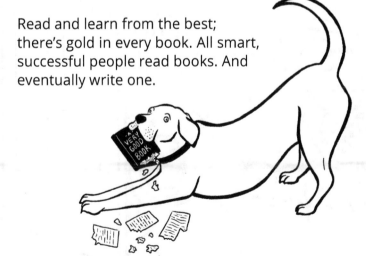

CREATIVITY OPENS DOORS

Singing, drawing, illustrating, writing, poetry, podcasting, photography, stand-up comedy, filming—your gateway to a global audience is through creativity and self-expression.

Don't suppress creativity—ever. It can be nerve-racking to put yourself out there for fear of judgement or being seen as "flighty" but once you let it flow and stop worrying about what your peers think, you will open the doors to success.

Start Now!

MAKE THE ASK

How did you get that person on your podcast?

We can't tell you how many times we were asked that question while we built our marketing podcast from scratch. Our answer was simple: "We asked."

Whatever you want in life, if you don't make the ask, you're never going to get an answer. Confront your fear of asking and never look back. This is an essential mindset that will put you on the road to success.

Think about the number of asks you get on any given day; don't you say no more often than yes? Then don't feel slighted when you get nos. The average in many industries is 99 nos for every yes.

But when those yeses come, THEY. ARE. FIRE.

START WITH A BLANK CANVAS

Think of your life as a blank canvas that can't wait for you to paint it with your next big idea.

Don't do stuff because your parents, friends, or colleagues tell you to follow some predestined path in life.

Follow the path you choose.

You'll hit many speedbumps, but isn't the road less travelled the more exciting way to live?

INVEST IN YOURSELF AND YOUR TEAM

When you're building your business, live within your means. That new car and fancy vacation can wait. Don't be frivolous and materialistic.

This doesn't mean you shouldn't enjoy life. Please ensure you enjoy life—you only get one. Just remember that every dollar spent elsewhere could be fueling your business growth.

We encourage you to adopt our mindset and think of money as the tool it is. Reinvest profits in yourself and your team, whether by finding a coach, taking new courses, spending money on new software and technologies, or building out a sales or business development team. (When you add to your sales team, the business will move and grow faster.)

The best decision we ever made was to hire a business coach. At the time, we had to choose between withdrawing the money to give ourselves a bonus or spending it on a business coach. Because we chose to hire the coach we did, our agency revenues grew by 50 percent in one year.

One of the most powerful realizations you can have is that by hiring a team, you no longer have only eight hours in a day and 40 hours in your workweek. With the right systems and processes and, say, five team members, you have 40 hours every day and over 200 hours every week to build and scale your business.

DO WHATEVER
IT TAKES
TO KEEP GOING

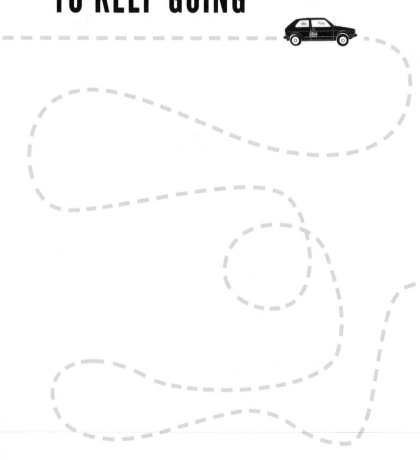

Living in his car that fall was not the plan. Jairus had rented an apartment for the next college year but on move-in day, he discovered the entire back wall of his apartment was completely covered with black mould.

The next morning, and every morning for the next two months, he and his girlfriend ate, slept, brushed their teeth, and got dressed in their tiny Volkswagen Golf parked in a grocery store lot (some of the worst sleep of their lives!). It felt like forever before they found a new place and got their lives back on track.

At the time, he would have traded everything for a roof over their heads. But after reflection, he realized he had gained new perspective and no longer takes things for granted. Today, if our colleague could go back in time, he wouldn't change a thing.

Always have hope. Things do get better.

DAVID BEATS GOLIATH

Don't be intimidated by the Goliaths. Respect them, yes. They are definitely a formidable force, having accomplished much.

But it's a big misconception that David can't beat Goliath.

Davids win all the time. Uber and Lyft upended the taxi industry. Amazon bypassed bricks and mortar retail for online shopping, while Airbnb offered cozy alternatives to sterile hotel rooms.

Beating the Goliaths of the world takes tremendous resilience, innovation, good timing, and a little luck.

Underdogs do win.
People root for them.
Be the next David.

DROP THE DEAD WEIGHT

"You are the average of the five people you spend the most time with." — *Jim Rohn*

If you aspire to greater things, to grow personally and professionally, it's absolutely vital to audit your circle of friends. Do they share your optimism? Are they driven to learn, work, and improve their lives? Are they driven by the same values as you are?

If your people are all negative and full of cynicism and angst they will, no doubt, bring you down. You can try to convert them to optimism, hope, and positivity but you might just have to trade some (or all) of them for like-minded people who push you forward, not hold you back.

Wondering how you'll ever find a new circle of people? Great question. Luckily, today's technology makes it easy to find and connect with new people.

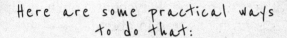

Here are some practical ways
to do that:

- Find an online business mastermind group in your area of expertise or in an area you want to master. Early in StudioPTBO's history, we were fortunate to join a community of marketing agency owners who helped keep us focused and gave us the sound advice we needed to grow.

- Subscribe to more podcasts and invest in more courses. Many thought leaders have virtual communities where you can connect with like-minded people.

- Volunteer in your local business community or non-profit. We have found that some of the best relationships are fostered through service.

BE RESILIENT

Top athletes, business tycoons, philanthropists and CEOs have this trait in abundance—incredible resilience. Resilience is the capacity to recover quickly from difficulties.

Successful entrepreneurs like Phil Knight, founder of Nike, didn't build a worldwide brand overnight. He struggled and overcame year after year of setbacks and enormous hurdles, but he kept at it. Read his memoir, *Shoe Dog*.

Steve Jobs was fired from the company he co-founded, but came back to save Apple and realize much greater success than ever before. Elon Musk of Tesla and SpaceX is another great example of resilience and overturning convention.

Be resourceful, steadfast, tough, and determined. Each failure will bring you one step closer to success if you just keep going.

Be resilient—always.

LEARN TO BE ADAPTABLE

This book was written during a pandemic. Countries were basically locked down. Everyone wore a face mask everywhere. Companies large and small went belly up and millions of people lost their jobs.

Industries were completely disrupted; sectors from hospitality to travel were impacted in dramatic ways; others had to pivot bigtime to survive.

Our agency was able to shift quickly from survive mode to thrive mode because we had the right mindset and business blueprint. Not only did we keep our agency afloat and meet our payroll, but we prospered and scaled up.

Our business strategy makes a significant difference for our clients: We empower passionate and energetic entrepreneurs around the world to shift decisively from bricks and mortar retail to online sales.

Anchored by a clear sales plan and an automated marketing system, we prospered during a worldwide pandemic.

Mindset
NOTES

LIFE

BE NICE
TO YOUR WAITER

Consider this: If you're not nice to your waiter, then to whom are you being nice? Service people should not have to suffer fools gladly (especially those with a few drinks in them), so don't be one of them.

And guess what? Your waiter is going to be a business owner, CEO, doctor, or lawyer one day and when your paths cross, they'll remember you.

Call it the law of reciprocity, the Golden Rule, or just plain karma: Treating others as you would like to be treated is absolutely the foundation for a happy and meaningful life, not to mention a growing business.

While this principle is not new, common sense isn't always common practice. Apply the Golden Rule to every moment you're interacting with another human being. Be nice.

TRUTH *Common sense isn't always common practice.*

FIND
YOUR FUEL

Find your oxygen in life and have at it.

Are you fueled by running, skydiving, marathon, hiking? Are you energized by big ideas, challenging problems, out-of-the-box thinking? Or does creating, drawing, sewing, sculpting, woodworking energize you? Or a combination of the above?

It's vital you do those things that bring you joy and fulfillment. These activities are the fuel you need to live your best life.

The gifts you give yourself enable you to contribute to others. Embrace them.

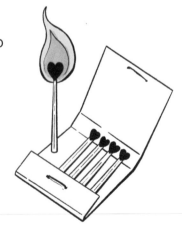

FIND YOUR HAPPINESS NOW

Be happy while you're living, for you're a long time dead.
— Scottish proverb

Well, write THAT at the very top of your whiteboard. This proverb doesn't mean you should live a life of complete decadence and selfishness. It means you should enjoy things in moderation and strive for contentment and satisfaction. Enjoy that quality steak from the fancy neighbourhood butcher. Taste some expensive vino.

Go to that fancy all-inclusive in the Bahamas. Belly laugh at that politically incorrect comedian without regret. Be happy you gave that homeless person $20. And don't pass judgement on what they might do with the money. Enjoy getting coffee for the person in line behind you. Smile about it.

Point is: Don't wait until retirement to find your happiness, because you might not make it that long or even find it then. Smile now. Live now. The idea is to die having lived a happy and fulfilled life, not regretting what you missed.

CREATE YOUR PURPOSE

Deep down in our core, human beings seek only a few fundamentals—purpose and fulfillment.

Purpose means different things to different people but at its core, purpose is the reason we exist.

Have you ever asked yourself, What is my purpose? The answer to this deep, philosophical question is foundational to both your personal and professional life.

Cody has wrestled with his purpose for a large portion of his life and career. It's what led him into his studies for pastoral ministry. But in the end, the study of purpose is what sparked Cody's passion for marketing and entrepreneurship.

He had served in a large telecom corporation for ten years. But his innate sense of purpose and desire to make a greater contribution in the world inspired Cody to head out on his own, to follow what he felt gave his life meaning and purpose.

Maybe you haven't found your "thing" yet or maybe you don't feel like you're living a purposeful life.

After having so many conversations around purpose, one thing is clear: Purpose is created and it's a choice.

We implore you to ask yourself a few questions. What is it that motivates me? What is it that excites me? What is the one thing that drives me to wake up every morning full of excitement and joy?

Life is too finite and valuable not to act on those things that bring you true joy and fulfillment.

Go. Create your purpose.

LIVE YOUR VALUES

Everything we do in life and business is motivated by our value systems. Even when we're not aware, our values shape and direct us.

Without personal values, it's almost impossible to become the person we aim to be.

Without business values, it's hard to actualize the business we are aiming to build and the culture we are looking to create.

Tony Robbins says that understanding how to build a value system for life and business begins with understanding our core beliefs. Why? Because our beliefs create our thoughts, and our thoughts ultimately dictate our actions.

This is why it's so important to block out adequate time to reflect on your personal beliefs, personal values and who you want to become. We recommend taking one full day.

The same is true for your business. Set aside time with your leadership team to thoughtfully identify the key values you will build your company upon and the vision that will guide its direction.

Once you understand the person you want to be, the organization you want to build, and the people you want in it, repetition and reinforcement will establish and strengthen those commitments to yourself. Find ways to repeat and reinforce your core values daily. Set up daily reminders inside your work chat and on your phone, talk about those values in your daily team meetings, and celebrate when someone in the organization demonstrates living their values. It all starts with values and beliefs.

Success is not overtaken by chasing an outcome; rather, success is found in chasing the person we need to become to achieve that outcome.

EMBRACE
THE MOMENTS

Everyday moments are fleeting. Embrace them. That Sunday morning canoe ride. The Baltimore oriole at your bird feeder. The big client you just closed. The champion soccer team you coached.

Breathe them in.

These moments are the memories you'll treasure when you become old, wise, and nostalgic.

CREATE YOUR LEGACY

You are building your legacy every day, whether you're aware or not. Now is the time to think about it—now, when you're building and scaling your business. Carefully choose the impact you want to make, the lasting imprint you want to leave behind.

Actualize your legacy vision with your team every day by sharing who you are, demonstrating your values as you deal with people, and living your company's mission. Your legacy-in-the-making can be a daily touchstone. Write these three questions on your whiteboard and revisit them each and every day:

- Why am I so passionate about my work?

- Whom do I serve?

- How am I doing my work with integrity and passion?

BE NOSTALGIC BUT MOVE ON

Neil was a magazine editor for 20 years and loved every minute of it. But as digital media began to replace print media in his field of communications and advertising, he was willing and excited to step into a new career as a business owner.

As entrepreneurs, we must adapt to each new era as technology and business evolve, or risk being outdated and left behind. It doesn't matter who you are or how long you've been in business; everything is always being disrupted.

Be nostalgic about the past, but don't get stuck there. How it used to be is over. Embrace the new era with excitement and vigour.

GIVE THANKS

The year after the Toronto Raptors won the NBA championship in 2019, Neil met one of their assistant coaches in a Quebec City hotel. (The Raptors were in training camp.)

After a great conversation in the hotel lobby, the busy coach hooked him up with tickets to the Raptors' scrimmage at Laval University. This amazing guy made Neil's day with his act of kindness.

Big moments come in small moments. Have gratitude for them and give thanks.

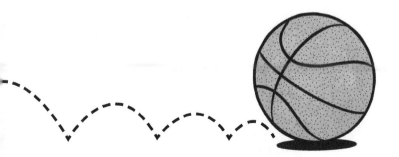

BE

Build a honey empire of kindness and empathy.

People are drawn to a work culture that is fun, engaging, generous, and open. One where everyone has a voice and an opportunity to contribute and collaborate.

Even at those difficult times when employees need to make improvements or be let go, demonstrating candour is an essential part of being nice.

Certainly, history gives us umpteen examples of how you can win by being a mean person and a bully. But wouldn't you rather win by being nice?

BE AUTHENTIC BY BEING YOU

Want to impress people? Don't try to be someone you're not. Be you. Be comfortable in your own skin. There is only one you on this planet (until science and technology make cloning possible).

The authentic you will attract authentic people and repel poseurs. (You really don't want to hang out with them anyway!)

FEED THE HOMELESS

When Neil was in his twenties, he volunteered at a Toronto soup kitchen through two chilly winters. That experience still shapes his life today.

Working in the kitchen, preparing meals, serving and interacting with the people awakened deep empathy and compassion in Neil.

He got to know many of the homeless people who, by dint of some combination of childhood trauma, bad luck, unemployment or addiction, ended up living on the streets or in shelters. They wanted the things we all want: a home, a job, a family, and children, which many had lost along the way.

Pushing yourself way outside your comfort zone opens you up to new perspectives and new insights. It gives you room to think about what you have and takes the focus off what you lack.

JUST BECAUSE YOU CAN, DOESN'T MEAN YOU SHOULD

Don't let material things define you. Success is not about having the fanciest car, most expensive watch, or biggest house in the most upscale neighbourhood. These things are nice, but not essential.

True success is being a leader in your business, family, and community; providing for people; giving back and paying it forward; being a philanthropist. These are the reasons people will remember you.

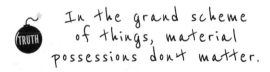

In the grand scheme of things, material possessions don't matter.

LIVE AN ALTRUISTIC LIFE

Kick that *What's in it for me?* ethos to the curb. After all, what kind of life are you living and leaving if it's all about you?

Giving back and having selfless concern for others will change your life. It's a remarkable feeling that will have a lasting impact on you and everyone in your world.

Day by day, inspire people, be there for them, listen, help, care, give a damn. Live the blueprint of the altruist. It will come back around to you, multiplied. It's called karma.

ENJOY THE RIDE

Don't romanticize owning and running a business. You'll have great moments, days, weeks, and months—and real lows as well.

Business goes through ups and downs and sharp turns. Something important we've learned along the way is to stay calm and work steadily through both the highs and lows.

THE WORLD IS MESSY SOMETIMES

Listen: Life is not always tidy. There is no such thing as perfection, although we reach for it continuously. That goes for business, too.

To keep pushing forward and making progress, you have to roll up your sleeves and get messy fixing problems. To keep or increase your momentum, you must be nimble and learn to improvise on the fly.

You may have to make quick decisions about employees (hire slow, fire fast), cut your overhead expenses, increase your expenses to scale up, call out your business partner or team.

It's all part of staying on course toward your goals.

HAVE A PLEASANT RESTING FACE

First impressions count—in seconds.

Do you have a resting bitch face? Catch yourself in the mirror as you walk by. What is your habitual, unedited expression?

Ask people for their honest opinion. What does your face look like when they walk into the room?

A pleasant, happy, relaxed, friendly, resting face makes a world of difference. Work on that version of your beautiful face.

QUALITY INPUTS = QUALITY OUTPUTS

It all matters—who you spend time with; what you read, watch, and think; what you eat; and what you do for physical activity.

You can measure the quality of the nutrition you give your mind, body, and soul by the quality of the energy you generate for the things that lift you up.

High-performance coach Brendon Burchard says,

"A power plant doesn't have energy. It generates energy."

So, what are those inputs that get your power plant humming and generate energy for you? Maybe it's getting on that treadmill, listening to uplifting podcasts, praying or meditating five minutes a day, or reading ten pages of a personal development book.

Start here: Discover the combination of inputs that will help you show up at your best.

The only way to generate quality positive energy is by controlling the inputs.

LATHER IN SELF-AWARENESS

Self-awareness is a greatly underrated skill. Most people are lousy at self-reflection, at understanding who they are, how their behavior impacts others, and how others view them.

Don't delude yourself. Your natural inclination is to be defensive, but you're not always right. Own that. It takes a big person to admit they are sucking the air out of the room, are a terrible listener, aren't good at helping others, aren't being a team player.

Developing the habit of continual, careful self-evaluation will lead to amazing self-improvement. In the process, you'll become more likeable, not to mention a much greater asset to those around you.

LEARN
THE HISTORY

To know where you're going, you have to know and understand history.

Perspective is one essential lesson history teaches. At 30,000 feet, history is cyclical. Periods of prosperity follow recessions; periods of calm and stability follow political upheaval. In this way and many others, history provides the context for the decisions you will make.

Read history books. Watch historical documentaries. Listen to podcasts on business, wars, culture, society.

Wise decisions informed by history will get you through the bad times and help you embrace the good times.

REVIEW YOUR GAME TAPES

All the great entrepreneurs, coaches, athletes, and salespeople scrutinize their game tapes to pinpoint their mistakes, identify what they could have done differently, and plan ways to improve.

Those insights lead to tweaks in their daily practice sessions—be it reps and quarterback sacks or content and delivery—so they perform better the very next game day and are positioned to make dramatic improvements over time.

Make your own game tapes by recording your client meetings, sales calls, media appearances, and internal team huddles. Watch and share them with your team members. Take notes, grade yourself and your team, and make adjustments that will position everyone to perform better.

For example, in the marketing world, something as small as varying the cadence of your voice can make a huge difference in perceived credibility and increased impact.

Regularly reviewing delivery, efficiency, and approach will reap huge rewards.

ACUMEN REQUIRES PRACTICE

Basketball icons like Michael Jordan, Kobe Bryant, and LeBron James have demonstrated astonishing acumen on the basketball court. They didn't have to analyze their options: *Should I make that cross-court pass now?* or *Should I take that shot?*

Decades of practice and study taught them to make split-second decisions that made them, their teammates, and their teams great.

Be thoughtful about the decisions you make, but make them quickly and own them.

Indecisiveness leads to malaise, paralysis, and stagnancy in your business.

If you practice like a champion, your ability to make accurate judgements and quick decisions will get better and better.

Think of great acumen like that.

TRUE LEADERSHIP IS SERVANTHOOD

One of the most important lessons we have learned while building our team is that true leadership is servanthood.

Managers have people who work for them. Leaders have people whom they serve.

One of the reasons we value our weekly one-on-one coaching sessions is the frequent opportunity to help each team member become the best version of themselves. They also give each team member an opportunity to give their perspective and honest feedback about the company.

Following are the three questions we ask weekly. They derive from a servant leader's perspective of What do you need from me? and How can I better support you?

- What is one thing you wish we would start doing?

- What is one thing you wish we would stop doing?

- What is one thing you hope we will continue to do?

Maybe you're asking yourself, How do I become a good leader? Well, another thing we've learned along the way is that good leaders create other leaders. Provide your team members with opportunities to grow, coach them as they take on leadership roles, and you'll find you have become a better leader in the process.

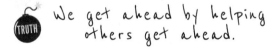

We get ahead by helping others get ahead.

DON'T TRUST YOUR MEMORY

What's the importance of a notepad? During an interview with serial entrepreneur David Meltzer (former CEO of the renowned Leigh Steinberg Sports & Entertainment agency that inspired the movie "Jerry Maguire"), Cody asked him how he retains and acts on the enormous amount of new information he continually receives. His advice?

"Don't trust your senses or memory, because they suck. They don't tell you the information as it is."

David then taught our podcast listeners the importance of writing down key lessons, stories, and action items as well as recording voice notes.

You see, when you have the mindset of a lifelong learner, you're actively listening, observing, and gathering nuggets of information everywhere you go. Some nuggets may be useful now, others in the future; some may be mildly interesting and some may be life-changing. Even if you don't quite comprehend their importance in the moment, the important thing is to record the information for future access.

How best can we retain that information and act on it? First, always be curious, never stop learning. Second, make it your daily practice to listen, observe, write notes, re-read your notes, and reflect.

Be old school—bring a notepad with you everywhere. Whether you're alone at a coffee shop, visiting with your grandmother, or listening to a podcast, take notes about the moments that inspire you. If an idea comes to you in a dream in the middle of the night, that's cool. Wake up and type it into your phone.

Capture your ideas and inspirations. They may be the seeds of a future business, book, screenplay, or a brilliant breakthrough.

Once you experience the value of note taking, you may graduate to journaling about your days, say, when you're building a startup. Your journal then becomes a neat piece of history for you, your family, and friends to look back on. And for you and your old colleagues when you reminisce about that iconic brand you built.

Who knows? Your journal just may turn into a business book that inspires millions.

OWN YOUR MISTAKES

By nature, humans make excuses and blame others for their own wrongdoings. Don't be delusional about your missteps and bad judgments. Owning your slips-ups, mistakes, and transgressions will change everything, including your guilty conscience.

Apologize and do what you can to make things right. If the person won't forgive you, so be it. Don't dwell, just learn from it.

Owning your mistakes has another benefit: improved relationships with your partner, kids, colleagues, clients, and customers.

WHY DUMB QUESTIONS ARE SMART QUESTIONS

Most people are scared to ask questions for fear others will think they're dumb. In fact, this was a big struggle for Cody during his first year as an entrepreneur. He hesitated to ask questions and that hampered his growth.

Then he realized the only way to learn, to seek more information, to solve issues, and to progress is to ask seemingly dumb questions.

We believe one of the main reasons people fail is because they don't ask enough questions. If you really think about it, sometimes dumb questions are the smartest questions because they're the ones people never ask.

WHAT ARE YOUR SUPERPOWERS?

Do people say you are really nice or an empathetic listener? That you have a great laugh, voice, or a perfect disposition? Or you're the best organizer, project manager, or sounding board?

Well, that's one of your superpowers.

Your superpowers are those gifts and talents that make you extra valuable at work and in life. Lock onto those superpowers, understand their value to you and to the marketplace, and make them work for you.

Superpowers don't have to be extraordinary and dramatic. Truth is that many people don't recognize their own superpowers because they've been using them all their lives. They often discount their value, not understanding that others would be thrilled to have the same superpowers.

Own your superpowers.
They will get you far in life.

EQ TOPS IQ

It's terrific you graduated from that Ivy League school with the highest GPA in your class. But are you personable, honest, compassionate? Optimistic, loyal, empathetic? Do you laugh? Who are you as a human being?

Stephen Covey, the late American educator, author, and keynote speaker said,

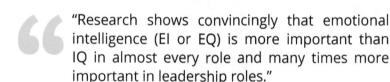

"Research shows convincingly that emotional intelligence (EI or EQ) is more important than IQ in almost every role and many times more important in leadership roles."

EQ is the ability to identify, assess, and control your own emotions and be sensitive to the emotions of others, while IQ is the measure of a person's relative intelligence. Emotional Quotient is what truly matters when hiring people and building a team.

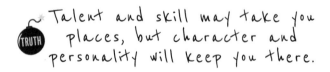

TRUTH — Talent and skill may take you places, but character and personality will keep you there.

HOW TO FIND INSPIRATION

Some mornings, you just want to crawl back into bed. That's life: You're not always going to feel 100 percent.

When we're off our game, here are four ways we find inspiration.

Interrupt your pattern
Do something out of the blue: Take a drive down a country road, get a spontaneous massage, or shut it down and go to the golf course. It's often the pattern interrupts that reignite inspiration in us.

Shift into learning mode
Learning new information is one of the fastest paths to fresh inspiration. Read a biography or watch an inspiring video about someone or something extraordinary.

Be with inspirational people
Spend quality time with people who inspire you. Seek out others who have a wide variety of expertise and experience to enrich your thinking and broaden your viewpoints. Their input and influence will fuel your personal and professional breakthroughs.

Think, reflect, and journal daily

Start by keeping score. How can you know how much momentum you have and if you are living an inspired life unless you are keeping score?

Your daily reflection time can be compared to athletes reviewing their game tapes. They analyze their performance in specific games, determine the ways they need to improve, and plan how they will get to the next level.

Reflecting and journaling allow you to look back and think about your state of mind during a certain season of life. They also allow you to examine how you felt in that peak moment or during that day you just weren't feeling it.

You can't measure what you don't track.

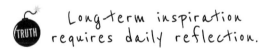

Long-term inspiration requires daily reflection.

Life
NOTES

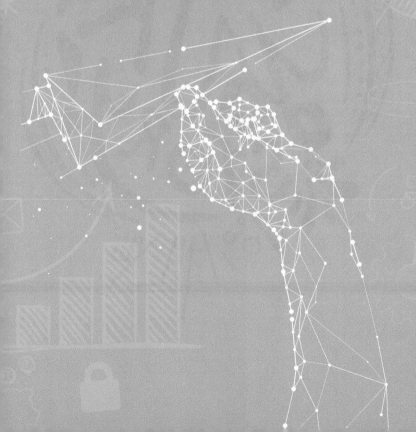

BUSINESS

YOU ARE A BRAND

Just a few short years ago, only businesses and organizations had brands. But now, through the power of storytelling on social media, individuals recognize they are a brand too, and their brand is instrumental in attracting consumers, clients, fans, and gigs.

So, it's time to build your brand on the socials in your entrepreneurial sphere. Find the way you communicate best on each platform—written, audio, video—then create content that speaks to your ideal customer. Whatever medium you choose, be authentic, be you. YOU are the brand.

Lather, rinse, and repeat these four words: I Am a Brand.

BE A *Positive* DISRUPTOR

The biggest shifts in business happen because people identify voids in the marketplace and innovate to fill them. Apple, Uber, Spotify, Airbnb, Netflix, Amazon, and Tesla revolutionized the marketplace, in spite of the skeptics.

Be ahead of the curve. You be the disruptor, shake up the status quo, make the changes that push your business, community, and organization forward. Go get it.

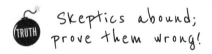

TRUTH Skeptics abound; prove them wrong!

TAKE YOUR SHOT

Our advice to entrepreneurs and innovators who are working to get a project off the ground is *Take your best shot.* It's the only way to get better at business and at life.

Don't hesitate because you're afraid to miss. Believe in yourself and take your shot. And if you do miss, figure out how to be better next time; recalibrate and try again, but at least take the shot.

When Jenish was an artillery man in Kyrgyzstan, that's exactly what they taught him. (He's now our colleague.) Aim as best you can, knowing your first round is going to miss the target. Your missed shots offer the data you need to calibrate your next few shots.

Keep at it until you hit your target.

HOW TO GET
RADICAL CLARITY

Your goals. Your mission. Your values. Your vision. Your objectives. Your milestones. Your projections. Each of these defines, shapes, and guides the day-to-day operations of your business and influences the direction of your life.

If you want radical clarity about where you're going, write it out on a whiteboard. The act of writing helps you externalize the internal and gives you new insights into yourself. Reading your own words helps you analyze the way you are leading yourself, your family, and your team towards success.

If used properly, your whiteboard can become a map to all that you treasure. Move one into your office and schedule time daily to write and scribble on it, update it and ponder it. Make it the focal point and repository of your best thinking.

SHARE YOUR VISION AND MISSION STATEMENT

In his book, *Start with Why*, Simon Sinek brilliantly states that every influential leader and every great movement started with the question Why?

Understanding the purpose and mission of your company is vital to its success because a shared vision will move your leaders and team members forward together.

Create a tagline that conveys the essence of your business, what you do, who you serve, and the brand experience you want your customers to have. You'll use it everywhere—on your social media platforms, in your bio, in networking conversations, and at events.

Prominently display your company's vision, mission statement, tagline, and business values on your whiteboard. Revisit them frequently as a team, even if you're a team of one in the beginning. They are the foundation upon which you will build, scale, and add infrastructure.

MAKE RELATIONSHIPS YOUR FOCAL POINT

We're not talking romantic relationships, we're talking business relationships: the relationships you build with colleagues, on boards, at networking events, online.

Neil and Cody have interviewed some of the most inspiring and successful entrepreneurs around the globe; all agree that each connection you make multiplies the size of your network.

Not only are you building new friendships and business opportunities with every new person you meet, but you can also introduce them to each other.

THE CONSUMER IS IN THE DRIVER'S SEAT

You can research everything about your customer down to their favourite colour of nail polish and then promote and advertise until the cows come home, but if consumers aren't buying your products and services, that tells you almost everything you need to know.

Yes, definitely try tweaking your messaging and positioning, but don't exhaust your team over a product or service line no one wants.

Recognize failure early and cut your losses; no excuses needed. Ditch it and move on. Focus on the products and services that are selling, the ones your customers do want.

Remember, consumers are the boss. They dictate the winners and losers—not you.

EMBRACE COMMUNITY

Community is everything, especially when you are building a business. Want a shot at going global? Start local with the people you know, the businesses you work with, and the connections you have. Make the most of them.

Do a favour, call in a favour. Reciprocate. Volunteer, donate your time and expertise to a cause. Serve on boards. Give.

Building a business is not solely about bottom-line profit. It should also be about making a greater contribution to your community, the lives of those you employ, and the causes near and dear to your heart.

The more money you make, the more impact you can have on your community.

TO GROW, SPREAD THE WEALTH

The mental shift from *I'll just do it myself* to *My team is my greatest asset* is not an easy transition to make.

When you're just starting out, you may have to do everything yourself. That hustle culture of 80-hour workweeks may enable you to reach new levels of growth, but don't stick with that. You will burn out and so will everyone around you—and that will slow your business growth.

Neil learned a less painful way to grow his media company (one of his early businesses) thanks to his friend and mentor, Stuart Harrison.

"If you want to experience growth, learn how to spread the wealth," Stuart advised.

To Neil and Cody, Stuart's principle means the pace of business growth depends first, on the number of tasks you delegate to skilled team members and second, on how much of the resulting "found" time is devoted to business-building activities.

Said another way, money is a tool that allows you to:

- Buy time for priority tasks and relationships
- Accelerate your pace and get more done
- Make a positive impact on team members' lives
- Devote more time to business-building
- Multiply your results by working in your zone of genius as much as possible.

We've really embraced the principle of spreading the wealth and it has had a big impact on us and on how we approach business.

In practice, it has allowed us to leverage our time and skills to do more faster, and to focus on activities that move the needle. Our results include accelerated business growth and enhanced quality and quantity of projects. In short: the more tasks you delegate, the faster you will grow.

We encourage you to spread the wealth in your business and enjoy the payoff in personal, professional, and leadership growth.

BE AN EARLY ADOPTER

Delusion can be a driving force for innovation. One of our favourite quotes comes from Russ Diemon's book, *It's All in Your Head.*

"Everything is unrealistic, until it's not."

People laughed at Jeff Bezos' idea for Amazon. It was unrealistic—until it happened. Now, millions shop on Amazon every day. What many thought was delusional turned out to be one of the greatest innovations of our generation.

If you look at iconic brands such as Amazon, Netflix, Nike, and Apple, they all needed early adopters to spur them on and to create tipping points as the masses followed suit.

Be an early adopter. Get behind someone else's idea if you like it. Be a customer. Refer others to them. Support their success.

Be loud and passionate about what you like. You will need to attract early adopters for your own launches.

OPPORTUNITY KNOCKS

Most people don't apply what they learn at professional training, even if they're still high a week after returning from a star-studded motivational conference.

That, right there, is your competitive advantage.

You are a doer, while the others are just talking about what they're going to do. This means that you have many more opportunities to succeed.

Memento Mori.

Go. Do with conviction.

Door artwork by: Jason Wilkins

AUTOMATING IS AUTO-MAGIC

What Cody learned at a Brendon Burchard seminar in California changed his life—and radically changed our agency's business operations.

Brendon challenged the entrepreneurs to pinpoint what was hampering their business growth and then taught them three ways to grow faster: automate, delegate, and remove all activities from your life and business that don't move the needle.

So, what did Cody do? When he returned from the conference, he began to automate, delegate, and remove all activities from inside our business that didn't move the needle.

Let's talk first about automation, because it offers so many ways to make your life and business easier and more efficient. For example, eliminate the back-and-forth with prospective clients by using an online booking calendar; automate your follow-up strategy with an email drip campaign; prevent key tasks from falling through the cracks by setting reminders on your phone. Automation can be auto-magic.

For those tasks you can't automate digitally, we encourage you to delegate. (Think of it as human automation.) Hire that virtual or in-house assistant to free up your valuable time.

Which weekly and monthly tasks could you delegate and how much time could you recover? Even if you freed up just 1-2 hours a week, you would have an extra 4-8 hours a month. What could you create with that extra time? What important projects could you tackle? And how far could you move the needle with that extra time?

Go forth, automate, and delegate.

CASH FLOW IS KING

Early on, we were lucky to have an accountant who helped us understand that cash flow should be our #1 priority.

Robert Gauvreau, author of *The Wealthy Entrepreneur,* is that accountant and our good friend and client. He knows from long experience that most businesses fail because they run out of cash. And yes, even highly profitable businesses can have insufficient cash flow.

Obsess about cash flow from this moment on. Write your revenue and profit targets at the top of your whiteboard and stay on top of them minute by minute, day by day. Be sure you create a contingency account. Set a goal and save toward it regularly, because rainy days will come.

Get the tools and support you need. Subscribe to an online resource such as QuickBooks or hire an accountant to help you with cash-flow planning and teach you what you need to know.

Because without cash flow—including reserves for a rainy day—you have no business.

HOW STICKY ARE YOU?

When you have a sticky tagline, slogan, or campaign that really resonates with consumers, like the famous taglines below, you are on your way to becoming top-of-mind in your sector.

"Think different."
"Just do it."
"It tastes awful. And it works."
"Betcha can't eat just one!"
"The Quicker Picker Upper."
"Where's the beef?"

Be bold in your marketing. Find a sticky tagline for your brand.

CONNECT WITH YOUR ♥ BRAND

Sure, you want to fulfill a need with your product or service, but you also want your customers to connect emotionally with your brand.

The Apple iPhone is a perfect example of powerful brand connection. From the first launch until today's generation, people can't live without their iPhone—it's literally attached to their hip.

How do you cultivate that kind of attachment and loyalty to your product or service, especially when consumers have so many choices?

The glue that connects you to your customer and your customer to your brand is your relatability, authenticity, cool factor, unique selling proposition, and stellar customer service.

DON'T BE BUSY

You can work hard all you want but if you're always saying, "I'm so busy," then you're doing something wrong.

Busy implies organized chaos, flying by the seat of your pants, running on a hamster wheel. Busy implies that you aren't organized and don't have enough structure or support.

Free up your time by automating and delegating, and then focus on the important activities that will build your business.

Be productive and efficient—not busy.

BE A CHANGE AGENT

Be the one who makes change happen in your organization. Be the one who influences and pushes for change and innovation. Greenlight ideas.

Don't sit back or play politics, because fence-sitters never prosper. Don't accept being stagnant or toeing the status quo.

If you aren't moving the needle, it might be time to move on.

FREE YOURSELF

Don't follow traditional rules of engagement without tracking whether they are getting results for you and your company.

If your advertising isn't generating revenue, tweak it or overhaul it. If your standard operating procedures aren't set up to deliver excellent customer service, change them. If your sales scripts are no longer converting leads into customers, get new sales scripts and new training.

Don't fall victim to the "This is the way we've always done it mentality." Free yourself from industry norms.

CREATE CUSTOMER SERVICE MOMENTS

When Neil was a novice boater, he took his Boston Whaler into a marina (his third after bad experiences at two others) to troubleshoot and fix a problem he had when starting his boat.

Turned out there wasn't really a problem. The marina mechanic took the time to show Neil how to start his boat correctly, without being condescending or making him feel dumb.

That marina gained a customer for life.

Explain how stuff works to your customers in a patient and concise manner. Remember—no one has as much subject matter expertise in your sector as you do. If you share that expertise generously with your clients and treat them with compassion and empathy, you will build loyalty, gain customers, and reap referrals.

BE MEMORABLE

Great marketing = great theatre = memorability.

Even if yours is an everyday product or service it has the potential to be memorable.

James Dyson proved this marketing truth—and the robust quality and durability of his product—by literally throwing a Dyson vacuum down a stairway at a PR event. Thus, he also proved the words "unforgettable" and "vacuum cleaner" belong in the same sentence.

That bit of theatre is one of Neil's fave marketing moments, witnessed at a Toronto public relations event years ago.

Create memorable moments for consumers that speak the truth of your brand and they'll never forget your products or you.

STAR IN YOUR ROLE

You may not have the goods to be the CEO, star basketball player, lead actor, top chef. But that doesn't mean you can't be a star.

Supporting roles are often the most vital ones in life and business because they are the glue that holds the entire team together. Unheralded roles are still hero roles. Where would Batman be without Robin and Albert? Michael Jordan without Scottie Pippen?

Strive to be the best sidekick and team member possible—and you will crush it in life.

Star in your role, as only you can.

DON'T MISS DEADLINES—EVER

Missing your deadlines is unprofessional, sloppy, and undisciplined. This applies to both internal and external projects.

Show them how it's done: Meet all of your own deadlines and reinforce this mindset daily with your team. Some may need a little help to break this bad habit, but it will be easier when you provide the processes and automation they need to be on time.

Clients will not be back if you miss their deadlines.

HAVE QUALITY TEAM MEETINGS

We continually tweak the timing, structure, and process of our meetings to ensure they are one of the most energizing and productive parts of the day.

To see what other businesses are doing and to get ideas for our agency, Neil sat in on a To the Point meeting at an architectural firm. (Their leaders also meet with their team every day to keep everyone on track.)

What we've learned is that frequent meets are best. We recommend you meet with your team daily and weekly to talk wins, life, strategy, timelines, prospects, low-hanging fruit, and to exchange ideas. Don't limit yourselves to production meets; also have creative meets to generate new ideas.

Set your team up for successful meets, too, by demonstrating and teaching them how to do it well and efficiently. Be sure to set an agenda and timeline. Assign one person on your team to lead the meeting and another to take notes.

Below are three types of team meetings that work well for us.

Daily Team Meeting

When: Daily, at the same time

Length: 10-20 minutes

Attendees: All team members (and no one is late)

Agenda: Everyone chats about wins, what they accomplished yesterday and what they will accomplish today.

Purpose: Leaders gain insight into areas of opportunity and ensure team members have everything they need to be successful in their daily work.

Weekly Departmental Production Meeting

When: First day of every week at the same time

Length: 60 minutes

Attendees: Department leads and all members of each department

Agenda: Discuss wins, bottlenecks, processes, and production plans for the week.

Purpose: Each department has an opportunity to discuss client wins and issues in more depth. The department leader can also address any changes to internal standard operating procedures and any team concerns.

One-on-One Coaching Sessions

When: Weekly at the same time

Length: 30 minutes

Attendees: Leaders and individual team member

Agenda: Team member completes a self-rating review prior to the meeting. During the meeting, wins and opportunities for growth are discussed.

Purpose: Gives leaders crucial information on how every team member is contributing to your business and whether they are working on the most important tasks in a rapidly changing environment. What might have been important last week might not be important this week.

No outs. Schedule your meets, have them regularly, and get the maximum value from each.

CREATE CHEMISTRY

Be the person who creates chemistry, a constitution of understanding and empathy. Be the person who brings people together and finds solutions to problems. Be the mediator in office squabbles.

Be that person, not the one who pours fuel on the fire and enables a toxic environment.

OVER-COMMUNICATE

A few years ago, we scheduled a client meeting to discuss an upcoming video shoot. Right on time, we arrived at the client's office—exactly when the client arrived at our office.

What went wrong? No excuses; it was our mistake. "We will meet you here," is not crystal clear. Where is here?

Don't just communicate, over-communicate. It will save you time, money, and embarrassment.

DON'T WING IT

Don't wing it through life, because you'll never build enough momentum to jump to the next level. You'll be perpetually stuck in the mud and everyone around you will know it.

Have a plan, a structure, a routine. Plan your days, your weeks, your weekends, your months, and years. Map out the steps of your plan with your notepad and calendar, making sure to give yourself adequate time to implement each one. Doing this will give you the best opportunity to actualize your plans.

"Most people don't plan to fail, they fail to plan."
—*John J. Beckley*

COLLABORATE EVERYDAY

When isolated in your silo, you feel like you're competing with everything and everyone, and you will miss out on most of the opportunities.

Conversely, when you collaborate with your team members, external organizations, and professional networks, your business and community will grow and prosper organically.

The DNA of every successful company and community is woven by collaboration, internal and external.

115

ASK FOR REFERRALS

There is no better public relations and marketing fuel than organic recommendations and referrals.

If you've done great work, ask your clients for recommendations and referrals. You're missing a huge opportunity if you don't. Most will be flattered that you asked, which will increase their investment in your brand.

Recommendations give your website, campaigns, and reputation added credibility and currency.

Client referrals to new prospects can directly increase your revenue growth, so create a process and reward system that will maximize the referrals you receive. It can be as simple as giving your clients a referral fee on every closed sale.

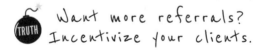

Want more referrals? Incentivize your clients.

PUBLIC RELATIONS IS GOLD

Entrepreneur and public relations expert Peter Shankman told us his greatest PR story when he was a guest on our podcast.

At the end of a very long day, Peter was boarding his flight home on a very empty stomach. Jokingly, he fired off a tweet asking Morton's Steakhouse (where he was a frequent customer) to meet him at the Newark airport with a porterhouse steak.

Guess what? Morton's Steakhouse was there with his porterhouse when he landed. Imagine the effort that went into making that moment special. What a stellar example of customer service and savvy public relations. As you would expect, both the tweet and story went viral, a goldmine of free public relations.

If you care about your customers like Morton's does, it's going to come back around in spades—and steaks.

FIND THE PR GOLD IN YOUR NEIGHBOURHOOD

You don't have to be a national brand to generate goodwill and grow your fan base. Neil has this great customer service story to share about one of our local restaurants.

I have been a fan of Gerti's Pub in Peterborough, Canada for a long time. Recently, when I called in to order I mentioned to the owner how much I missed their Pollo Pesto sandwich that is no longer on the menu.

So, what did they do? A couple of days later, they surprised me by dropping off my old fave sandwich. A kind, yummy gesture I won't forget that further endears Gerti's to my heart...and tummy.

I shared my experience on social media and now in this book to give Gerti's some well-earned PR and appreciation.

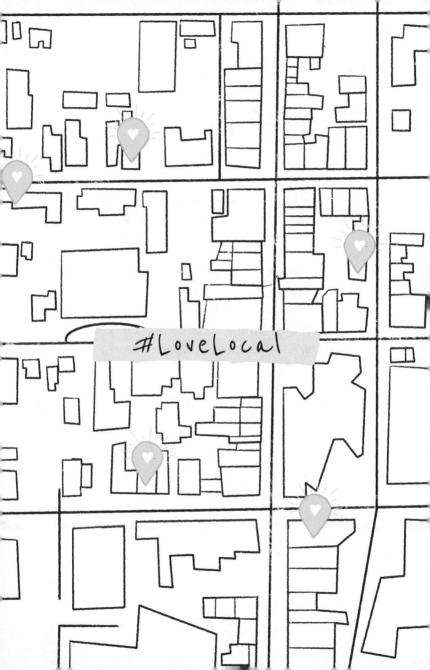

#LoveLocal

AUTOPILOT IS NOT YOUR FRIEND

Don't coast. Don't get stagnant. If you are on autopilot, be self-aware and understand the impact coasting is having on your life and business.

Don't stay stuck. It's absolutely all right to have a bad day. You just never want that bad day to turn into a bad week, month, quarter, or year. Get out of the funk by pivoting or tweaking or refining what you're doing.

One of the main reasons we implemented end-of-day reports for every team member in our business is to avoid autopilot. End-of-day reports create daily momentum and accountability, both personally and professionally. No outs—it's way too easy to shift to autopilot when you are not keeping score of the game of life and business daily.

End-of-day reports will help you check in and stay on track. Ask yourself key questions such as:

Did I protect my health today?
Did I protect my calendar?
Did I block out time for key tasks?
Did I work on things that matter today?
Am I on pace to hit my goals for the week, month, and quarter?

Our end-of-day report has helped everyone on our team perform at higher levels. In fact, one of our team members excelled quickly inside our organization by using it. This team member had a high-performance structure in their professional life, but not in their personal life. So, they sought out a life and fitness coach, practiced accountability, and used a variation of the end-of-day report in their personal life.

In less than nine months, they embodied daily high performance and accountability and were leading our entire team as an account director.

If you want to perform at a higher level, you may also want to take actions like these: hire a coach, entrust a friend, colleague, or family member to be your accountability partner, implement end-of-day reports, or join a business mastermind group.

KNOW WHEN TO SAY YES

Say yes to the job you covet or that board seat you've always wanted. Not because you think you're supposed to, but because it's the right decision for you at the right time. There's a huge distinction between the two.

Learning to say no keeps you from overextending yourself and making decisions you'll regret once the euphoria of saying yes wears off.

Buyer's remorse happens in business, too, when we make hasty decisions that weren't right in the first place. Due diligence, always.

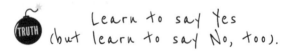

TRUTH Learn to say Yes (but learn to say No, too).

GOOD RELATIONSHIPS ARE THE GLUE OF SUCCESS

Be obsessed with the data that reveals the health of your business, but be equally obsessed with forging emotional connections with your team.

Nurture your relationships. Check in with your teammates regularly, ask them how they're doing, and ask how you can help them succeed. We check in every week with every team member. Even 15 to 30 minutes a week is enough.

What gets scheduled gets accomplished. Scheduling and consistent follow-through with weekly check-ins gives your team members an opportunity to have a voice and to make an impact.

Keep at it and your employee retention will be sky high, your teammates will be happy and work better, and your human resources specialist will appreciate you all the more.

KEEP RETENTION TOP OF MIND

Businesses work for years to crack the code that converts leads to customers. When that moment arrives and you've landed a new client, celebrate. But truly, this is when the work of growing a business, client-by-client, begins.

Entrepreneur Alex Charfen created a model that maps out five key functions of growing a business: lead generation, lead nurture, conversion, delivery, retention and upsell.

Alex considers delivery, retention, and upselling to be the most important functions to sustained business growth. We agree, and they are always top of mind at our agency.

We distinctly remember learning how marketing agencies are perceived from the other side of the desk, thanks to David Morton, former CEO of Quaker Oats Canada and Neil's dad.

David told us the two biggest reasons marketing agencies get fired are failure to drive results and lack of communication.

- Delivering on what you promised and getting results for your clients are key requirements for retention.

- Excellent communication is absolutely crucial in any client-facing business. If you're not communicating with your clients on a daily or at least weekly basis, you are vulnerable.

When communication is frequent and effective and relationships are thriving, it's a lot easier to sell additional services to your clients. If you are performing for your clients, the fastest way to continue to grow is by introducing new products and services that will benefit them.

CREATE AN IRRESISTIBLE OFFER

Acquiring new clients is always more expensive and time-consuming than selling your additional services to current customers and asking them for client referrals. That said, acquiring new clients is an absolutely vital part of growing and scaling a business.

Want to cut down your customer acquisition cost? Create an irresistible offer. How, you ask?

Let's face it: no amount of marketing or traffic can overcome a shitty offer such as discovery calls and minimal discounts. That's what everyone does.

Knowing that your offer can make or break your marketing campaign, go big and up the ante. Consider offering a 50 percent discount on their first order; stack value by adding a second or third service to your original offer; or craft a guarantee that outweighs the risk of taking action.

In our case, we were guaranteeing leads like every other agency. So, we created an irresistible offer— guaranteed booked appointments.

The result? Simply by changing our offer from 50+ leads to 10+ guaranteed booked appointments, we dropped our agency lead generation cost from $130 to $14 per lead.

GET AWAY
FROM YOUR DESK

If you can't see the forest for the trees, interrupt your thought pattern by taking a walk outside.

You don't need a destination. Just walk by yourself, with your business partner, or select team members. Breathe deeply, discuss the problem, and you'll gain some clarity.

A few years ago, we got bogged down while building our own agency's new website. We had held multiple meetings to discuss the website's look and feel and our process, but weren't getting anywhere. Months passed with no progress.

Then one day, we went for a coffee walk with our designers. That was the turning point. That conversation clarified why we were struggling—we had been completely overthinking our agency's project in a way we never did for client projects.

We decided then and there to refocus the website on our key business principles, strip everything down, and declutter its look and feel. We launched a new website that was more robust, less bloated, and did a much better job communicating who we are and what we do.

The next time you're spinning your wheels or your brain is stuck, get up and get some oxygen to refresh your brain.

BE EFFICIENT

Get to the point. Don't take an hour for a meeting if you need only 20 minutes.

Always be ready with your agenda, a firm schedule, and a thoughtful plan of attack. Just like a sports team, have your drills mapped out in advance, because people need structure and tactics.

Always be as efficient as you possibly can. You will make great advancements in your business and personal life and truly feel you have accomplished something purposeful, intentional, meaningful.

YOU ARE QUOTABLE, TOO

Become a thought leader yourself—be that luminary who shares their expertise on radio, podcasts, blogs, TV, who writes book forewords and endorsements, and is invited to give TED Talks.

Why not you? No one is quotable until they are.

SPEAK UP, SPEAK OUT

Whenever you get the chance to speak in front of people, whether it's a handful or hundreds, take it.

Public speaking is like speed dating for business. You're building your brand, starting a relationship with every person in your audience, and attracting potential new clients.

Speaking on a subject you are passionate about is exhilarating. As with anything, the more you do it the better you'll perform and the fewer jitters you'll have.

Use cue cards to keep you on track; avoid reading from a script or teleprompter. As you become more comfortable, ditch the notes altogether. This doesn't mean wing it or blue-sky it and provide little or no value. Ditching the cue cards means you've mastered your presentation—after practicing in front of the mirror, your peers, your partner, and then a live audience.

Remember to record and review your "game tapes"; filming your practice sessions is an invaluable method for improving your live performance.

Allow time for Q&A at the end, always. Some of your most meaningful connections with your audience can result from these personal exchanges.

Film your live speeches, too, so you can evaluate yourself afterward—your vocal inflections, your posture and gestures, and the words and expressions you stumble on, like um and ah.

Public speaking will expand your reach exponentially. Give it a go.

GET OFF THE FENCE

Fence-sitters don't necessarily lose at life, but they don't win either. If you sit back and say nothing, don't act on your feelings, or don't pursue your passion for fear of others' judgement, you are only holding yourself back.

If you really think about it, you're likely holding others back, too. Instead, take a stand for what's important to you. That will spur them to act, too.

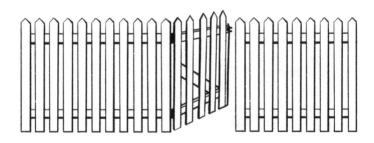

SELL ETHICALLY

Have you ever felt misled or lied to during a sales interaction? Maybe you were purchasing a new car and saw through the sales pitch.

Luckily, early in his sales management career at Best Buy, Cody's manager gave him excellent advice that he still lives by today: It's best to under-promise and over-deliver.

Keep the best interests of your customers at heart. Do the right thing for them. Be moral. Sell with respect, humility, and integrity.

While it's ideal to sell a product or service you believe in, what's most important is that you sell it the right way. Your rewards will be enduring customer relationships, quality referrals, and a retention rate that's through the roof.

HIRE PEOPLE WHO HELP YOU WIN

This is where self-awareness truly kicks in: are you thinking about hiring that person because their skillset doesn't threaten you and your area of responsibility? If so—don't.

Hire people who can:

- Become better than you.

- Make your business stronger.

- Challenge you, push you, innovate with you.

Don't hire inferior people because of your own insecurities. Shaq and Kobe won three NBA titles with the Los Angeles Lakers by challenging each other and having healthy competition. There was no Shaq without Kobe, and no Kobe without Shaq.

Find your next champion to help take you and your business to the next level.

DON'T IGNORE LOW-HANGING FRUIT

That next big client, next big scorer on your soccer team, next best friend, next soul mate, next employee—sometimes the people you want are right in front of you, but you don't see them.

That coveted outside hire you're courting may be tempting, but what about the person who has been working right alongside you, who has proven their loyalty and resilience?

If you're being honest, haven't you been grooming them for this moment all along?

BEING IMITATED AIN'T BAD

Imitation is, indeed, a sincere form of flattery. When we're young and deciding who we want to become, we naturally model our actions after those who inspire us.

So, if someone is mirroring your actions and words, don't be offended by it. Be confident and appreciate that you have become a leader and mentor for others.

INSPIRE MENTEES TO BECOME MENTORS

Neil was once Cody's mentor. Then they became equals. And now, Cody mentors others.

This is how true mentorship works: The mentee eventually climbs the mountain, becomes the mentor's equal and begins to mentor others. It's a beautiful thing to behold.

Be a mentor to your kids, your grandkids. Be a mentor to your colleagues. Be a mentor to people in your entrepreneurial ecosystem.

Inspire possibility in all of them. Teach them about opportunities, business acumen, leadership, money. Be a sounding board.

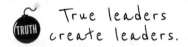 True leaders create leaders.

YOU CAN BUILD MANY MORE

You probably know several serial entrepreneurs. There are good reasons they have more than one company; after building their first, they got the urge for that adrenaline rush and started another.

Also, it was easier to build a second or third business because they had created a transferable business model.

Look at everything you learned from building your first business: how to hire, train, supervise a team, and create the culture; how to build the infrastructure, automate tasks, and manage cash flow. You also developed your EQ on the rollercoaster ride and endured the trials and tribulations of business ownership. And you not only prospered, but learned to thrive while having autonomy and running your own business.

And now, you have the business principles, operations knowledge, and the strength to transfer to a new business. Go get it.

THE SCORE IS TIED WITH 3 MINUTES LEFT

To hit milestones, you must set concrete goals and be motivated to reach them. Pretend it's a tie game in your favourite sport, things are down to the wire, and it's go time.

All the foundation blocks you've laid, the team building you've done, and the strategies and tactics you've practiced have prepared you for this moment.

Now, close that sale, land that client, hit that million-dollar mark in revenue. It's there for the taking. Get it.

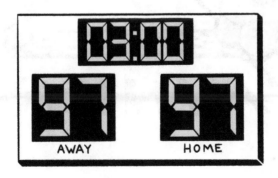

SEE YOU AT
THE FINISH LINE

You have to believe you're going to win—or you won't.

Life is a continual series of challenges that will test you again and again.

If your mindset isn't dialed to "winner" mode, you stand no chance, whether it's a client presentation, poker game, or tennis match.

You must believe this: *When others see me and my business, they see greatness.*

Even when you lose a challenge, and we all do, your drive to win will soon have you crossing the finish line first.

Earn the miles by giving it your all—always.

Business
NOTES

ACKNOWLEDGMENTS

ACKNOWLEDGMENTS

Thanks to our fantastic publishing consultant, Susie Schaefer, and editor Bonnie McDermid—we fondly call them Book Angels—for stewarding us through this process. What a dynamic duo!

Thanks to the extraordinary David Meltzer for being a guest on our podcast and writing the inspiring foreword to our book. We completely align with your life's mission to empower over ONE BILLION people to be happy.

Thanks to our StudioPTBO partner, Nora Mickee, our all-star designers on the book, Adam McKinlay and Emma Deugo, and our dream team, including Jairus Leeson, Shannon Schutt, Jenish Odigski, Jeremy Biden, Reilly Porter, Camila Rebour, Aldo Feoli, Austin Flowers, and Christine Roberts.

Thanks to Stuart Harrison for his mentorship and candour over the years.

Big thanks to Robert Gauvreau for his financial coaching and expertise in helping us build and scale StudioPTBO the right way.

Thanks to Belinda "Unstoppable" Ginter for her mindset coaching with us and our team.

Thanks to our Business Coaches Taki Moore and Bill Baren for their incredible guidance putting us on the right path to success.

Big thanks to Jeff Hohner for his wisdom, radical candour, and encouragement on our journey.

Thanks to all the members of our StudioPTBO Marketing, Mindset & Business Secrets Facebook group for their positivity, energy, and passion for entrepreneurship.

Thanks to all our podcast guests over the years who bet on us and themselves. We're all part of a unique entrepreneurial ecosystem where we understand each other and go after life and business.

Thanks to all those who bring hope and joy to the world. Empathy and kindness will always win.

ABOUT THE AUTHORS

Cody May is chief executive officer of StudioPTBO, a global marketing agency based in Peterborough, Canada, and co-host of the StudioPTBO podcast. Cody is an expert at paid advertising, sales and communications, and coaches entrepreneurs on those topics.

Cody's mission in business is to help over one million entrepreneurs experience passion and exuberant energy in both their personal and professional lives.

Neil Morton is the co-founder of StudioPTBO, a global marketing agency based in Peterborough, Canada. An expert in communications, marketing, advertising, social media, and branding, Neil honed his craft in Toronto where he was editor-in-chief of several magazines. He has appeared several times on national television and is a frequent speaker at industry and public events. He served as a campaign chair for the United Way Peterborough and District, and was on the Peterborough Chamber of Commerce board of directors.

In his spare time, he has a passion for volunteering, philanthropy, and the great Canadian outdoors—mainly cottaging and canoeing in the Kawarthas.

ABOUT StudioPTBO

Okay, so you've finished the book...now what?
Feel like you can go get it in business!?
Of course you do!!

Here are the superhero skills StudioPTBO provides for our passionate and energetic clients worldwide:

- **ATTRACT** new leads and acquire clients through online advertising and funnels while building a great reputation in the online space!

- **NURTURE** new leads and existing clients by being omnipresent online and using customized content to target your audience!

- **CONVERT** more prospects with the StudioPTBO Software, automated funnels, and our in-house call centre!

There are no limits to your potential!

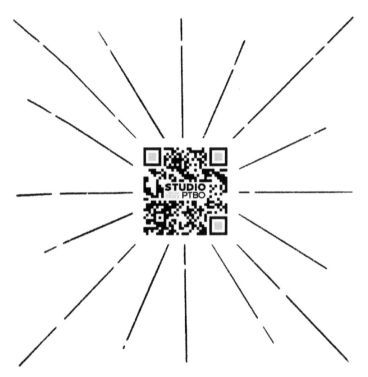

Scan the QR code to begin to change your
business (and life) for the better!

studioptbo.com/bonus

9 781777 554606